Nothing Resembles Me

By

Nahed Fraitekh

Nahed Fraitekh

Copyright © 2026 Nahed Fraitekh

All rights reserved.

Dedication

To my mother, whose love and support have always been my guiding light. Though she has passed, her presence remains with me in every word, in every canto, in every breath of this book. This epic is for her the eternal source of my strength, my first homeland, and my everlasting inspiration.

Nahed Fraitekh

Acknowledgment

This book is not only a collection of poems; it is the story of how I became a strong woman through trials, distance, and memory. It reflects the journey of transforming pain into beauty, absence into presence, and longing into freedom. By writing these hymns, I honour both my roots and my growth. I acknowledge that my strength comes from the very struggles that once threatened to break me, and I offer this epic as a voice for love, freedom, and the unyielding spirit of women everywhere.

Table of Contents

Nothing Resembles Me

Nahed Fraitekh

Invocation of the Eternal Flame

Before the cantos unfold, let the heavens bear witness.

I call upon the stars, the moon, the winds of memory,

to testify to a love that is both worship and rebellion,

both wound and salvation.

This book is not merely words,

but a temple of longing,

a kingdom of passion,

a mirror of the soul.

Here begins the journey of a voice

that bows only to God,

yet rises in song to love,

to freedom, to hope,

to the impossible that becomes eternal.

Let the reader enter with reverence,

for every canto is a flame,

and together they are a constellation.

Throne of Femininity

My lady,

my Lord created me to shake the throne of femininity with
my hands,

to place a rose upon sorrow's face.

My lady,

my Lord created me

to gather every share of beauty,

and to bless the one who multiplies my love beyond measure.

Lay your palms, my lady,

upon the Buddha's temple gate.

Feel the walls of a shrine so proud

they tremble before a single kiss

from your lips.

Give me your small fingers, my lady,

so I may trace with them a frightened heart,

silence breaths that fled before their time.

Give me your hands, my lady.

Come,

let us carve our beautiful memories into stone.

Let us laugh together until the echoes rise,

weep until the silence bends.

Perhaps our innocent love will plead for us,

Nahed Fraitekh

perhaps it will kneel in devotion,

perhaps it too has burned in passion's fire

as we have burned.

I write to you, lady of love,

to pour out what my soul cannot contain.

I do not fear love.

I fear only for you,

for the breaking of a tender heart.

I melt in longing,

I dissolve in desire,

yet still I do not confess.

I Was Created to Be Me

My Lord created me to be me.

My Lord shaped me to be none but I.

I was made to wipe my own tears with my hands,

to place myself in the path of every hardship,

to dissolve every impossibility that blocks my way.

I do not intend to draw nearer to myself,

yet my heart has changed its desire.

Love, O lady of passion, has taught me

to love without delay,

to let simple words lift me in joy,

to care more deeply for my own details.

It has driven me to seek a heart

whose pulse has altered,

a heart shaken by feelings,

that fell asleep within my embrace.

My longing awakened my heart from its slumber,

and my soul entered into a bond of love with my heart,

calling to a troubled pulse in the vein,

calling to a body wandering in pain, nothing more.

O my lady, I do not retreat from love except to love again.

I do not forget those I have loved except to love them more.

I do not avert my eyes from yours in fear,

but my vow is to love my heart first.

For my Lord created me to be myself.

I shall enter into a love affair with my own heart,

wander within the jewel of a love unveiled.

I shall love myself in every detail,

call my soul each night toward happiness,

and shower my spirit with a touch of clarity.

My heart has taught me, O my lady,

to melt in passion,

to love you without loving you,

to know you are mine and not mine.

For I am the one lost in pain,

the runner chasing his own heart,

the soul clinging to the desire of desirelessness.

There Is No Worship After the Worship of God

If we were created to worship God,

then permit me, my lady,

to name my longing for your eyes

a worship after the worship of God.

My love for you, as long as I live, will give me life,

melting me in passion, quenching me in desire.

I glimpse your walk from the corner of my eye,

and I resist the fire of yearning with my lids.

My heart trembles with love,

and I fear it may stop,

and with it, love may die.

A heart I cradle within my ribs,

protecting it as a mother shelters a lost child.

I stifle a voice that cries in anguish

from the torment of distance.

My soul has become, in the hands of God,

a wandering, straying spirit,

awaiting your steps,

wrung with longing for eyes

I have worshipped after the worship of God.

Eyes forbidden by passion to draw near,

yet they called to a soul to meet them.

But the soul refused, faltered, leaned upon itself,

and cried out in the agony of loss:

"There is no worship after the worship of God."

Nothing Resembles Me

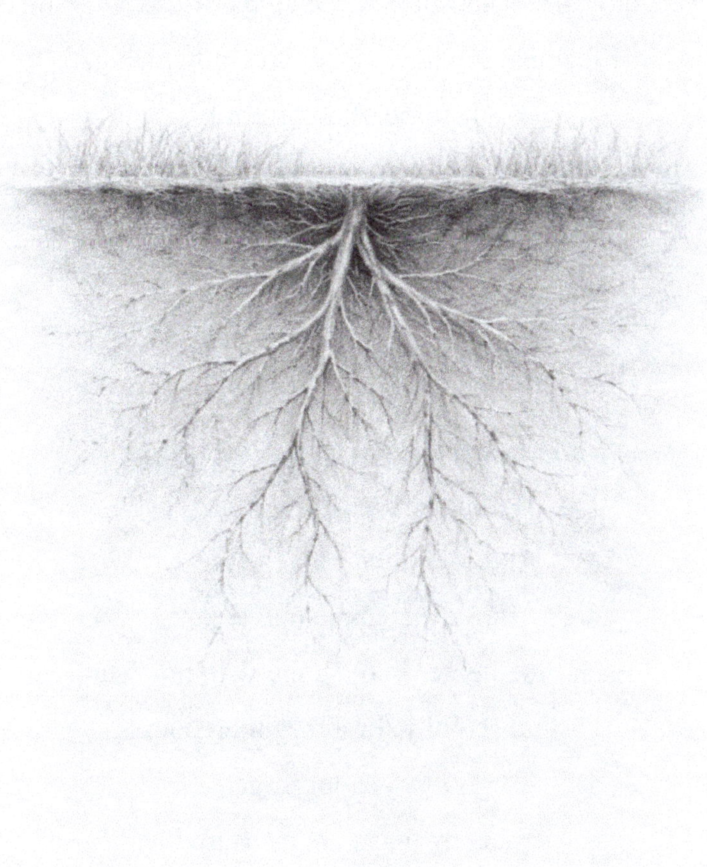

Nahed Fraitekh

Feelings

I feel that I was created on the day the universe was born,

the day our father Adam was created,

the day angels and stars revealed themselves to him.

I feel that my time is the time of hardship,

the time of no return,

the season of letters worn and fading.

I feel that I am that yearning human,

that soul inflamed with love for adventure,

love for words of passion and desire

that fill the earth and the two worlds.

That human who carries his spirit

upon drops of purity.

And each time I love myself,

I love the whole universe.

Each time I enter into a bond with my heart,

I find serenity for a forgotten body,

forgotten, yet not forgetful.

I feel my days are measured

by the count of years,

by the moments of happiness overflowing—

happiness of heart, of mind, of soul,

happiness of a body lost at evening,

Nothing Resembles Me

while the moon shines,
casting its beauty and radiance
upon the mirror of the flesh.
It wipes away with its light
the pain of impossible meetings,
and restores to the body
the love of tender fingers,
fingers that caress a restless body,
a body waiting, a spirit suspended,
neither rising to the heavens
nor descending to the earth.
That is the love of the impossible.

Nahed Fraitekh

My Solitude Comforts Me

My solitude comforts me,

for I cannot bear that my essence should love the impossible.

Your love has taught me to seek the difficult,

never to accept the little.

Each time I utter your name,

my blossoms are crowned,

and they exhale fragrance like the breezes of paradise.

Your love, my lady, has taught me never to say no,

to renew myself each day.

Your voice opens for me the gates of memory;

your whisper unlocks every guarded door.

Your love, my lady, has taught me

that the soul rises above the body,

that the heart rises above the mind.

It has taught me patience,

to endure the day in waiting.

It has taught me not to desire,

for desire may fade,

but your love is an eternal secret,

a flame that never dies.

I love myself, my lady, because I love you.

I delight in the torment of longing for your love.

Nothing Resembles Me

You are the spirit of the body,

the queen of queens,

the lady of princesses of passion.

Your love, my lady, has lit the universe for me,

and kindled arrows in my heart like shooting stars.

Your love, my lady, has quenched the fire of the flesh

with a pure love that accepts no challenge.

For I am the companion of my solitude,

and the lover of my own soul.

Nahed Fraitekh

Every End Has a Beginning

Every story ends only to begin another,

every night departs only for day to shine.

O my lady, I do not love you

with the worship of idols,

for idol worship is past,

while the worship of God is past, present, and future.

I do not dwell in the past,

but I journey toward the future,

a future where I seek you and myself.

O lady, I was created only to worship God,

and to love you after the love of God.

If I find you, I find love.

If I touch you, I find passion.

Your love fills me with life;

your passion fills my soul with clarity.

You, whose desire my heart has chosen,

make of my world a hope

that fills the universe.

I worship the God who created you

and created me to be,

to become the one faraway, yet ever close

for you, the near distant.

Nothing Resembles Me

My love for you, my lady,

is the mirror of my shadow,

my longing, my burning, my lament.

Your love is a rose whose colour and brilliance heal me,

yet whose thorns pierce me with pain.

Your love is a star suspended

between heaven and earth,

untouched by human,

unreached by spirit.

And I…

I was created to be a love wandering in pain.

For you, my lady, all love.

For you, O past that is present.

For you, O my present without future.

Nahed Fraitekh

By Your Life, Who Are You?

By your life, who are you,

and what is passion within your keeping?

By my life, I am but a passerby,

sewing desire as I please,

bowing before my heart

as you have willed for me.

My path is not easy,

nor can I endure the impossible.

I fashion from the threads of love a tapestry,

to offer it to you as the way.

I called you by the fairest names;

I sang to you my sweetest melodies.

I saw you strike the earth

to ascend toward the sky of love.

My longing for you stretched

from earth to heaven.

The pulses of my heart quicken

whenever the breezes of your fragrance rise,

crowned with the scent of jasmine.

Perhaps you will cast toward me

a glance of your eyes,

and in that moment, I shall feel

Nothing Resembles Me

that you are the way

that I may ascend with you

to the highest degrees of passion,

embracing a heart that gathered its breath

and was sealed by the fire of desire.

I shall hold a soul

that embraced me before our meeting,

that entered with me into a bond of pure love—

a love before which none bows

except those scorched by the fire of passion,

a passion unaware

that your passion is the impossible.

There Is No Prayer
Except for Your Eyes

There is no prayer except for your eyes.

I made ablution to pray two rak'ahs beside you;

I made ablution to pray two rak'ahs for you.

Your love inspired me with the path to paradise,

yet your passion struck my heart

more cruelly than Cain's murder of Abel.

By your life, I cherished mine only for you.

By your life, I loved desire,

and trembled, and burned in its fire,

all because of you.

I made ablution for a worship

in which you were a god enthroned upon my heart.

I made ablution for a worship

in which you were inspiration for a thousand tales,

in which you were passion, love, and pain.

I made ablution for a worship

where I bow only to your eyes,

and prostrate only before your hands.

Yet there is no bowing, no prostration, my lady,

except to the God who created your eyes

for another worship.

Nahed Fraitekh

A God who shaped your eyes

to reign upon the throne of love and desire,

to pour forth inspiration, longing, and femininity.

I bow only to the God who created you in perfection;

I prostrate only to the God

who fashioned the goddess of love

to take form in you, O lady of passion, my lady.

So let me, my lady, pray to eyes

slain by love, buried in folds of hope.

Let me pray to eyes created only for worship.

And is there worship greater

than the worship of your eyes?

Chaos of the Kingdom

My freedom is the chaos of my kingdom.

I play it as I will, not as it wills.

My freedom is my world,

and all that my hands have possessed.

I fashion it from the essence of words,

and I love it as the exile loves his homeland.

My freedom is an open book,

from which I feel no shame,

to which I give no heed.

My freedom is memories I have sung,

songs I have lived.

My freedom is myself, my pen, my letters.

My freedom is you, my lady,

and a hidden love,

neither rising to the surface

nor sinking to the depths.

My freedom is a moon shining

in a sky without stars.

And my sky shades me

with the shadow of letters enduring

as long as the universe endures.

It rises like a pure love,

defending, fighting, drawing near.

My love approaches you, my lady,

and stands at your barred gates.

For you, O lady of passion, are my freedom.

You are my kingdom,

and all words.

And I…

I am, my lady, the chaos beyond chaos.

I am the hardest of possibilities.

You Are Not What I See

You are not yourself when I see you.

You, with all that is within you,

are not as I see.

In distance you are beautiful;

in nearness, more beautiful still.

You are a secret in the heart never spoken,

and you, O lady of passion,

are farther than reach can grasp.

You hold in my soul a wish,

you hold in my heart a place.

Your love, my lady, is torment to the heart,

a sorrow that lingers.

I love you as much as Qays loved Layla,

as Antar loved Abla.

I love you as Adam loved Eve,

a love of existence itself

that cast them forth from heaven's paradise

into the paradise of life.

Together they walked in love and longing,

drawing nearer to one another still.

I love you as the heart loves

the breezes of first love,

and the ache of second love.

For you are the first love,

and you are my second love.

I do not play with words,

but my game is in glances.

When I see you, words scatter.

I turn away, close my eyes in escape…

and all the shades of winter flee from me.

Nothing Resembles Me

Nahed Fraitekh

My Gain and My World

You, my lady, are my gain and my world.

You are the first, and you are the last.

Your whispers are my words,

and your words are my pain.

You, my lady, are every possibility.

I have no strength without you,

and my life is eternal in your presence.

You, my lady, are my pain,

stretching to the planet Mars.

You are the rebel, the ruler, the tyrant.

To you belongs all my love;

to you my strength and my pride;

to you my passion and my melodies.

Whenever the world turns against me, I remember you.

And whenever I remember you,

my restless soul soars,

and all the black clouds scatter.

For you, my lady, are all love,

and that infinite hope.

If you are the world,

then the hereafter is but the extension

of my love for you,

Nothing Resembles Me

and the melody of my longing.

Remember me, my lady,

whenever the winds of November blow.

Do not grow still; do not forget me.

For your love is air,

its breeze amber,

its fragrance fierce, unbroken.

Nahed Fraitekh

I Coloured My Life with My Hands

Will you permit me, my lady,

to read to you what words may allow?

Will you permit me to sing for you

the fairest of songs?

I read to her some of my words;

I sang to her my feelings

with a trembling voice,

rising from the ruins of my being.

I scorched my heart with my own hands,

tormented my soul with countless sighs.

I gathered scattered letters

to fashion them into words—

words of love, of esteem, of friendship.

I coloured my life with my hands

and placed it in hers to read,

as I willed for her,

and as she herself willed.

I folded the fire of love within my heart,

and laid before her the paths of passion,

swaying between sighs and smiles.

I read to her stories twofold, threefold,

and by the tens.

Nothing Resembles Me

I shared with her my heart, my pen, my memories—
stories that passed as though life itself
were created to be between us
a handful of lessons.
The breezes of desire passed to extinguish
a love never meant to be,
a love created only to drag behind it
the wreckage of defeats.
So let the words of love die between us,
for who is worthy of such words?

Nahed Fraitekh

I Long for a Corner That Gathers Us

I long for a corner that gathers us,

for a moon that shadows our secrets,

for a tremor of love that fills our hearts.

I long for an evening when you were there,

when my embrace was warmth for you,

and I was there.

I long for a touch that crosses the horizons of my body,

that stirs my soul to trembling,

that scatters my mind,

that casts down my heart.

I long for a kiss that whispers in my ears

before it reaches my lips,

that sings to me songs of love, passion, and hope.

Fate taught me never to surrender,

yet to you I surrendered.

I gave you my soul and spirit;

my fragments clung to you.

We touched, we embraced, we promised.

We did not dwell long upon words,

for letters have another taste—

even their bitterness is sweet.

It was love, it was passion, it was hope.

Nothing Resembles Me

As though eternal love was created for us in moments,

as though the sighs of the world ended in whispers.

Words gathered us,

glances of love,

tears of longing.

It ended with nothing

but bitter memories.

I Thought We Had Met

I thought I had seen her and loved her.

I journeyed in my dreams, in pure illusion.

I loved, I complained,

I spent sleepless nights in sorrow.

I longed, I grew restless,

I whispered her name in secret.

I thought she had a name to be called.

I thought my name carried for her a melody,

that my time with her bore a price.

I felt, with all the love that possessed me,

that I was living the colours of the rainbow.

A butterfly awakened me from my slumber,

its wings radiant,

its hues mingled with the elegance of life.

I sensed the morning breeze and knew

I had never met her,

never known her by any name.

Her fragrance had never passed my door,

her shadow had never walked beside mine.

She was illusion, dream, and fantasy.

Nahed Fraitekh

Your Love Has No Limits

She whispered to me, the dark-haired one, and said:

"Your love has no limits.

You are my sky; you are my covering."

Her whispers ignited the fire of my longing,

stirred my yearning,

hardened my veins.

Her murmurs deepened my torment,

burned the pages of my patience.

She whispered to me, the dark-haired one, and said:

"In nearness you are mine,

in distance you are mine."

Her whispers rose in my ears,

her voice rose with my groaning.

Her murmurs echoed,

and my soul returned to them.

I whispered to the dark-haired one and said:

"Forgive me, for I have abandoned your love.

Forgive me if I no longer love you."

She whispered to me, saying:

"You were the tales,

you were all the love.

You were my poetry,

Nothing Resembles Me

and you became my departure.

You who were passion,

you who were my pure love.

I have wearied of the torment of your desire,

I have tired of longing for your meeting.

Depart from my memory,

leave my thoughts,

that I may gather the fragments of my mind,

and draw for my soul a future,

a brighter tomorrow."

Nahed Fraitekh

You Are My World

You are my world.

Life halted for me and refused to move.

I pleaded with it a thousand times and more,

I caressed it as passion caresses

the beloved of its lifetime.

I said to it: "O life, be my fairness,

for longing has slain me,

and love has betrayed me."

It refused, it grew arrogant,

and left me stumbling in my solitude.

I said: "What is life but a moment we steal?

What is life but passion,

whose taste is known only to those who love?"

And I loved,

and passion overtook me.

I grew accustomed to life as I willed it,

and I cast my world into the well of your love.

I bore witness that your love, my lady,

is the greatest spectrum of life.

With your passion my world halted,

bowed to you with those who bow,

prostrated before you with those who prostrate.

Nothing Resembles Me

From your love I received a command,

and you were its path.

You became all passion and its secret.

And then… only then…

I whispered to life your name in secret,

and it moved.

By God, had it not moved,

I would have called it by your name,

and made its sky a lover of your name.

For, my lady, life is nothing but you,

your name, and my love for you.

Distance of the Sky

I realised you are distant as the sky,

your heavens dim and black,

without moon, without stars.

Clouds heavy, their rain black,

piled, collapsing,

neither quenching thirst nor lasting.

I no longer see your smile,

nor imagine your face in morning or evening.

I see only a project of lies fallen.

Do not be angered if my honesty wounds you, my lady,

for I possess nothing but my pen and a few words.

Nahed Fraitekh

Long Was the Waiting

I stood at the gate of your paradise waiting.

I grew weary, hesitant, confused by love and fear.

My heart inspired me with passion and folded within itself

love, desire, peace, and longing.

You were the one I loved,

you were the one before whom I was defeated.

When love ends, when hope ends,

all words of longing and sorrow shatter.

Our voices turn toward the fate of the impossible,

our desires play upon the rope of passion.

I neither draw near to you, my lady, nor am I quenched.

Destiny pulled me toward your love,

yet you withdrew, scattered like autumn leaves,

carried by the winds of November.

Your love dwelt in my heart as the impossible,

and the pain of separation shook me,

with no alternative to hold.

Journey of Life

I walked into the desert of fatigue,

seeking love, trust, and hope.

I paused to recall a year gone by,

found life shifting, changing.

I tasted its sweetness bitter,

its bitterness sweet.

Experiences engulfed me in white and black.

My eyes shone with love and joy,

my heart wept with pain and longing.

Today I stand beneath the sky of hope.

I raise my hat to every soul that left a mark,

to all who passed through my life like strangers,

departing as migrants from their homeland.

I raise my hat to all who left an imprint,

who taught me to be stronger, to be myself.

I am a human ever seeking hope.

Life enticed me with its sweetness and bitterness,

its trials engulfed me harshly,

yet I succeeded with honours.

My Black Lily

You entered my life as a black lily.

My eyes adorned themselves with it at times,

at times struck by its darkness.

Its blackness lures the gazer,

yet drawing near burns the hearts of the regretful.

It hurled its darkness upon a sky once clear,

shook with its power the light of weeping stars.

I touched it, velvet, adorned,

yet its blackness harsher on the heart

than the cold of November.

Its chill lost the path of passion

between the peace of lovers.

It abandoned my tears alone in the night's darkness,

left my heart wandering, pale, uncared for.

It was she who taught me life's lessons with a blow,

that shook all my being.

Nahed Fraitekh

I Loved a Rose

I loved a rose neither red nor wine-coloured.

Its touch was silk, its thorns harmless.

A rose delicate, fragile, tender,

its petals freed like doves in flight.

Its fragrance flared like a breeze,

drifting upon the wings of clouds.

A rose I adored in weaving,

sang in hope.

But the arrows of its passion

killed my heart with sorrow.

It rejected my love,

confused my soul with pain and grief.

Its colours faded, its fragrance dried,

since it departed to a world

without love, without peace.

Whispers of a Rose

A rose whispered in my ear and said:

Rise, revolt, and shake the world.

You are not half the universe; you are the universe entire.

Plant love for yourself and reap its fruits.

Be a free woman, created for building, not for suffering.

Be strong, mighty, unconquerable.

Do not hesitate, do not falter.

Complete the path you chose, and that chose you.

Love yourself, bring it joy, never belittle it.

For you are everything, and everything is you.

How Can I Write Poetry?

How can I write poetry when you are not before me to hear it?

How can I praise hair, eyes, cheeks?

Where are you, my enchantress, my muse?

Where are you, the one my soul loved?

Where are you, my tomorrow, my present, my yesterday?

Where is my muse, whom I loved?

Where is my beloved, whom I befriended?

Where are you in my days, my joy, my dreams?

Where are you, for whom my soul was made to love?

Where are you, for whom my heartbeats sang of beauty,

for whom my eyes sparkled with joy at meeting?

You were promise, you were hope.

You departed, and with you departed

all meanings of life.

Nahed Fraitekh

I Shall Write Poetry

I shall write poetry and not care.

I arrange my words as I will,

hide within them a love that insists on being.

I shape words of love, of passion,

sometimes of sorrow.

I do not know if I praise her love,

or if in her passion I became imprisoned.

If I write my poetry upon the clouds, it rains,

and it lies upon the sun, moon, and stars to rest.

If I draw it upon the earth, it blossoms.

My poetry is like breezes of a phantom

travelling toward the clouds.

I shall write poetry in which I see your eyes.

I promise you will not see

how deluded I am in your love.

Poetry in which I paint eyes, cheeks, lips,

from whose lines fly strands of enamoured hair.

I shall adorn myself with the black of your hair,

fulfil a promise made to eyes

wearied by sorrow.

I shall travel in imagination

towards eternal paradise—

and what does eternal paradise endure

without your eyes?

I Rearranged My Papers

I rearranged my papers to suit my presence,

attended to my words to suit your absence more.

I lost my words in the sea of your passion,

forgot that I love myself more.

I cast my love upon the sand of a shore

without limit, without end.

I stood at the gate of your temple,

kneeling, pleading.

I stood at the gate of your temple

to pray two rak'ahs

for eyes that killed me twice.

I begged to forget you,

that forgetting might be my path to remember you.

If you pass through my mind, pass as a stranger.

If I pass through yours, close all your doors,

lock every open gate,

erase all illusions before me.

If I pass through your mind,

prepare all soldiers of death

to take me to my end,

to overturn all measures of love into ruin.

The Moon Was Gone

Night unfolded; the moon was gone.

It slipped from the arms of clouds and dissolved.

It is longing I possess,

it is infinite hope, it is torment.

She is the one with whom I could not endure,

and in her absence my heart melted.

I soared toward the sky of love like a butterfly,

eager, chasing waves of mirage,

hoping to find her phantom

swimming among forms of absence.

I returned along the paths of passion,

and passion fell into my heart's embrace,

a love rebellious as the clouds.

Nahed Fraitekh

You Were a Beacon, and Still, You Are

I long for you, O beacon, star of love and ruin.

A star in the night I adore,

whose love grows with each day.

You were a light that split my path,

and when you vanished, all secrets vanished with you.

Is it you of whom I speak?

Is it you whom the soul loves?

Is it you, or has the heart imagined?

You were a beacon and still are,

a star in the sky with a tale,

with an echo upon the earth,

upon my heart as at the beginning.

So rest, my star, in peace.

Bow with the stars of heaven,

prostrate in praise whenever I recall you,

your name, and the light.

When We Love

When we love, letters scatter,

words disperse.

When we love, we stammer,

forget ourselves and memories.

When we love, fate tosses us,

casts us upon its winds in exile.

When we love, we see the sparkle of passion in our eyes,

we see ourselves changed.

When we love, the world has no single meaning,

but all meanings gathered.

When we love, we do not choose,

we falter before choices day and night.

When we love, the body gathers its desire,

the heart feels its pulse and collapses.

When we love, we flee toward the impossible,

we lie, knowing we lie,

and invent no excuses.

You Are All Love

You are infinite love,

my passion stretching to Mars.

You are the air, the breezes of life.

You are words that restore life to life.

You are eyes that plant hope,

heartbeats that whisper your name in shyness.

You are all this and more.

And you ask me why all this love?

When I loved you, I was not alone,

but your love gave me strength.

I felt life in its finest adornments.

You ask me why all this love?

It is my love for you—

enough as life's elixir,

enough as a ring of salvation.

Nahed Fraitekh

Beautiful You Are

Beautiful you are in all you hold,

in all my heart's love and brilliance.

Beautiful you are in every detail,

beautiful in the measure of my love,

my devotion, my attachment.

Beautiful you are as land without desert,

as green homes stretching to the horizon.

Beautiful you are as breezes of a phantom

speaking your name.

Beautiful you are, my queen, my lady,

as a flower opening between the palms of a homeland,

as a migrant bird gathering its songs above horizons,

colouring your sky, the moon, the stars with your name.

Love Makes Me a Different Woman

Love changes me,

I know not who I am.

Love is a green carpet,

without mind, without eyes.

Love is a radiant smile,

devotion, madness.

Love took me from the not-I

to my world of I.

My wishes multiplied,

my memories turned.

I fell behind the world of reality

into a world of imagination far away—

a world without time, without hour,

without accounts, without trivialities,

a world filled with bouquets of wishes.

Love took me from the world of no passion

to passion.

It filled me with love of self,

so I could only love me.

I loved myself for myself,

ignored that once I loved another.

I did not hesitate long

before I recalculated.

I rebelled, I cried,

I called my pride.

I awakened myself from slumber

to welcome my brilliance,

the beauty of my soul.

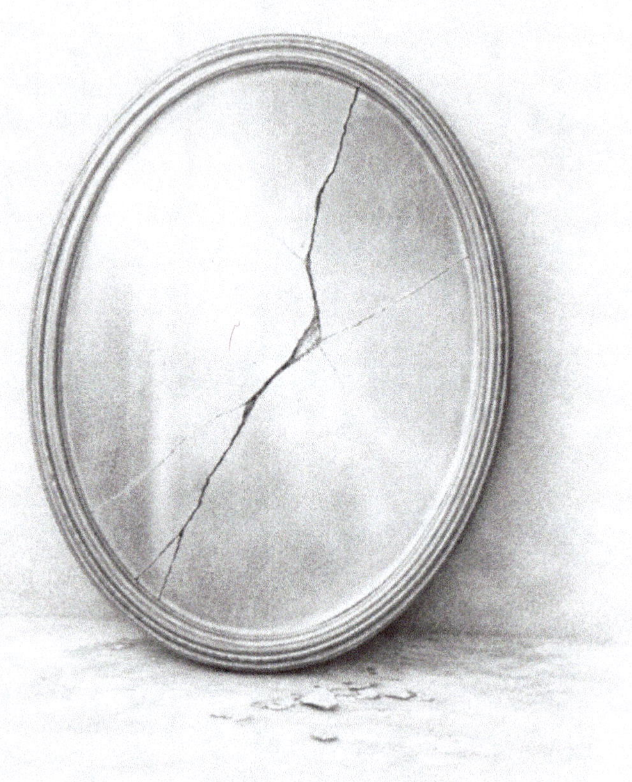

My Mirror

I sat before my mirror, gazing.

I found myself pale, silent, contemplative.

It asked me: What troubles you,

what wounds your heart?

I answered: It is the fire of longing and memories,

illusions of life, loss of hours.

It said: But life is beautiful for those who will it.

I answered, tears in my eyes, sighs in my breath.

I wished never to leave my mirror,

to remain in a world of wishes.

It said: Stretch your hands to me,

let us build a world unmatched.

Reality is fairer than a past gone and ended.

I answered, tears falling like rivers filling roads:

Come to me into the world of imagination,

a world without disappointment,

without burdens of trivialities.

Nahed Fraitekh

You Are My Phantom and Mirror

When I close my eyes, I see you.

When you close yours, you see me.

I see a love bewildered,

without path, without end.

You are my phantom,

you are my mirror.

I neither draw near nor depart.

I await my way to you, bewildered.

I give all generosity,

rebellious in your love.

I know your love is a lie,

I know I lie.

I play with memories,

change letters of words.

I seek a path leading to you,

draw a road beginning with you, ending with you.

You are my infinite road,

you are memories of the future.

Nothing Resembles Me

Nahed Fraitekh

Who Am I

Spare me the question.

I am the breath that broke against the teeth of silence.

I am eyes mapped by salt and shadow,

heavy with the cargo of a thousand sleepless nights.

I am love-unrefined, luminous, and wild.

I am the transparency that lives in the marrow of hope.

I am the friction where two oceans collide

but refuse to bleed into one another.

I am the infant's first jagged cry-

the sound that makes the world's pulse falter.

I am the one in whom the earth has lost its direction,

the one from whom the universe's language has fled.

How do you seek a road to me?

There is no trail that leads here, yet

I am the only bridge to the stars.

I am memory-the nectar and the blade.

I am the fever, and I am the cool hand that breaks it.

I am the tear that stays hidden behind a laugh,

and the one that collapses in the wreckage of grief.

I am a secret love, folded into the shrapnel of the bullet that
finally found my heart.

Nothing Resembles Me

For God's sake, stop asking.

I am the ghost of the years you've lived,

and the echo of the years you haven't met yet.

Nahed Fraitekh

I Lost My Way

I lost my way among memories and whispers.

Pictures drew me, songs enticed me.

I placed my soul upon the edge of an evening,

of fairest wishes.

I lost a wandering heart;

you were its hardest memory.

Wait, my beloved, do not leave the fields.

My morning is delayed,

the night of lovers unveiled.

Nights turned me, hardships possessed me.

How long I waited,

how I wished my dreams would stretch for hours.

Wait, my beloved, let us travel together

behind the fairest butterflies.

Let life hasten with us,

let memories triumph.

Wait, my beloved, do not leave the fairest times.

Enjoy the pulses of a heart living the moments.

Go Your Way

By your life, I loved in passion only your breath.

By your life, I wrote poetry only for you.

I felt no fragrance like that

which caresses strands of your hair.

For you I lay upon that cloud

hovering above your home,

awaiting what feelings you hid from me.

For you I stole some images

that represented your presence.

O distant near one!

Your existence means nothing to me now.

Your questions no longer matter,

your absence no longer pains.

My path is not yours,

my kindness does not comfort you.

You were lady of my passion, my life.

My obsession today is forgetting you.

By oath, you mean nothing to me now.

So go your way!

Nahed Fraitekh

Longing for the Past

I am a woman whose desire is desire,

whose passion is the sky of love and exile.

I am quenched only by longing,

I regret no love that passed,

that folded with time.

Longing for the past is not like longing for the past.

It fills us with passion and love,

it storms our hearts with storms.

I am all passion, all love.

If there is no hope in a clear sky,

there is no present, no past

for hearts empty of desire.

When we live pain twice,

we scarcely feel ourselves.

When we live pain each day,

our hearts die of anguish.

We scarcely perceive any feeling,

we wander between the sense of a loving heart

and the memory of a mind still recalling.

Nothing Resembles Me

Nahed Fraitekh

My Soul in Your Hands

If I gave you a choice in my love

between love, passion, desire:

If you chose love,

I would say: I love you

as wide as the universe,

as full as the world.

Love is only for you,

complete only with you.

If you chose passion,

I would say: I adore you in every detail,

your eyes, your soul.

In passion you are my inspiration,

my fire, my poetry.

If you chose desire,

I would say: desire is but love and passion,

and I desire nothing in this world but you.

You are my love, my passion,

you are all this and more.

My passion for you, lady of passion, kills me.

You are my killer,

you are the one who gives me life.

My Muse

My muse you are, distant yet near.

I gave you my love, my words.

I gave you my years, past and future.

With your words shatter

tales beautiful and sighs.

With you I am the not-I,

and I fashion myself as I am.

In your absence roses withered,

the moon's light died.

In your absence almond blossoms yellowed,

carnations died.

In your absence the universe ceased to turn,

and I wandered in the depths of forgetting.

I Loved You and Still Do

You are not mine,

as the world is not mine.

I suffered,

I learned not to ask for the impossible.

You are my impossible,

and still.

I loved you, and still.

You are my hope, my world,

my pen, my words.

You are past and present,

you are eternity.

I waited, longing for your eyes,

I descended in love for your lips.

I stood between past and past,

sat upon a rope of fate,

trusting in an old-new love.

My strength exhausted,

and still.

You are love of past renewed,

you are my destiny.

I sailed in the black of your eyes,

seeking hope, seeking bond.

Nahed Fraitekh

I found the past as past,

all present scattered.

I loved you, and still.

Who Is She?

They asked me: Who is she?

I faltered in answer,

my eyes faltered.

Hard to speak your name,

hard to reveal a hidden secret.

I sighed, paused, said:

A dark-eyed beauty.

Eyes adorned with black night,

mad night.

You whom I loved madly,

whose love filled my heart,

filled the universe.

Whose glance made me love life

as a mad lover.

Whose eyes filled my world

with love, desire, madness.

Your love, my lady, lit my universe,

gave me patience for life's hardships.

Are you asking me: Who is she?

She was illusion, wound, imprisoned dream.

A story ended,

with it ended all dreams.

Behind it dried wounds of heart,

tears of eyes.

Are you asking me: Who is she?

She is my beloved,

dark-eyed beauty.

Nothing Resembles Me

Nahed Fraitekh

Lessons of Life

I thought my heart full of all love.

I thought all love filled me.

I learned from you, lady, not to expect the impossible.

You taught me life does not stop for anyone.

You taught me not to collapse,

not to wait for dawn.

You taught me to race my shadow,

not the days.

You taught me not to trust,

not to confess.

People change; hearts shift.

You taught me to fold all pages of my book,

not to share my writings,

to close my door.

You taught me life is fleeting,

friendship not lasting.

You taught me not to tell tales,

for tales do not tell,

secrets do not forget.

Days do not stop for anyone.

Our Songs, Our Evenings

Our songs, our evenings, our present, our past—

memories that pass, make us laugh,

perhaps make us weep.

By our desire we recall the reasons.

We grow, yet childhood remains within us.

We steal moments to laugh;

we move, and time moves within us.

We may weep with joy,

laugh with sorrow.

Pain makes us weep,

pain brings forth joy.

We weep from the pain of separation,

we laugh at the pain of impossible meeting.

Scattered feelings,

love of self from the depth of anguish.

We grow accustomed to people in our lives,

forget those who once were all our life.

Friends come, others depart.

We grieve for the distant nearby,

care not for the near distant.

We travel within our solitude,

rebel against every impossible.

Perhaps we live as we desire,

and desire what we live.

Nahed Fraitekh

If My Heart Were Stone

Would that my heart were stone,

would that my poetry never was.

Let breath cease,

let feelings die.

Reckless emotions,

love fading like worship of idols.

My words falter before you,

I know not when my days end.

You were my utmost joy,

you became pain of meeting,

distance of sky.

I feel the strength of distance within me,

a wise decision of eternal departure.

Yet my heart hesitates,

the bond between us does not renew.

Nothing Resembles Me

Nahed Fraitekh

A Question to Myself

I questioned myself who I am,

I searched in the depths of soul for spirit.

Perhaps I find that little girl

whose dreams were chocolate,

whose joy was music.

That child who loved to gaze at stars,

wander with lights of planets hidden in clouds,

to write poetry hoping it sees light one day.

I did not find me.

I no longer know me,

no longer understand me.

I no longer own me,

I am not as I was.

Life misled me with its tricks.

I searched for me in remnants of memories,

found me hiding in the past's shadows,

clinging, refusing, defiant.

Dreaming only of what remains of memories,

hoping the past stays,

hoping all life's troubles die.

I Called You

I called you by my name,

I sang you, my pain.

I saw you in my dream,

a bird fluttering in my visions.

You flew far from my path,

made me weep.

My words travelled with you,

longing shook me, sighs.

O you whom I loved with all my being,

would that your name was my title,

your love my crown,

you, my time.

Nahed Fraitekh

My Paradise

I shall make you my paradise.

I shall embrace you and kiss you.

I shall fly with you above the clouds of my wandering
homeland.

No… my homeland is not lost.

It is I who am exiled, far beyond horizons,

I who have no homeland, no kin.

Nothing Resembles Me

Nahed Fraitekh

I Waited for You

I waited for you morning and evening.

Because I love you, I cannot help but love your earth and sky.

Yet you do not speak of passion,

you imprison the breath of love that rebels within you like a
raging storm.

You speak only in the fear of a woman slain by hiding her
love day and night.

Your wildness wasted longing and killed a heart that clung to
your soul with pride.

Come, Let Us Wander Together

Come, my beloved, let us wander where words themselves
are lost.

Come, let us flee behind the letters of love and sighs.

Let us search for a hope to accompany our days and smiles.

Come with me, let us leave the kingdom of earth

for the kingdom of heavens.

Let us roam among the spectres of stars and moons.

Come, my beautiful one, let us love our evenings and songs.

Let us rest together upon a horizon as distant as memories.

Nahed Fraitekh

My longing for you

My longing for you shook the wounds

My yearning overflowed upon all people.

I hide my pain in silence,

yet my soul desires only to be yours.

I am the breeze that touched her brow,

and the branches bowed in reverence.

My heart sat upon the throne of passion,

lost, waiting, silent in pride.

Nahed Fraitekh

Do You Remember?

Do you remember the old days,

when we stayed up late, sharing stories,

and endless laughter spread before us?

We shared the dreams of youth—were they as we wished,

or as the days decreed?

We dreamed of impossible hope,

and who but us loves the impossible?

The days pulled us, cast us into the depths of oblivion.

We found ourselves scattered dreams,

no stories to share, no illusions to hold.

Can roses regain their brilliance once they wither?

Autumn Time

It was autumn, and I awaited the winds to pass.

Time slipped away, and your fingers withdrew from the
strings.

What deceived you—the hardness of heart, the tears of eyes,
the stone?

Your breezes fell like leaves of trees,

scattered and dispersed like drops of rain.

September was the month of fate,

in which all tales withered, and the moon slept.

Nahed Fraitekh

I Adore Hope

I am a woman whose passion is hope,

whose love for life in you is unashamed.

I imagined love twice,

drowned in sorrow with two stars.

A star in heaven I loved,

another on earth I adored.

My heart killed me twice:

once when I loved you in silence,

fled my homeland seeking exile.

Today love killed me again,

driving me to seek exile within exile.

Remember me when November winds blow,

remember me when fate storms you.

Seek me in pictures—

memories; tear them, burn them,

cast them into fate's maze.

Kill me, my lady, kill my love again and again.

Burn my pictures, my memories, my hope.

Place me in folds of passion,

perhaps September winds touch my heart,

end the pain.

I loved you, lady, with all my weakness.

Nothing Resembles Me

I placed you in the fairest pictures—
pictures most beautiful, most noble, most sweet.
Pictures without beginning, without end.
Pictures fate lost,
lost with them all memory, all deceit.

Nahed Fraitekh

Of What Illusion Do I Speak

The days taught me not to expect much.

They taught me that what is in my hands today

is not mine tomorrow.

I learned from my haste to be patient,

from my feelings not to feel too much.

The passing of people through my life taught me

not to trust, to wait, to take heed.

Some friends taught me that friendship does not last,

that no one holds a place within the eyes.

Those I thought valued me taught me

to live reality, not dream.

They taught me that what comes quickly

goes swiftly.

They taught me to believe what I feel,

not to wait for the zero hour.

I learned that the only path is distance,

that my path is valuing myself more.

Nahed Fraitekh

Life Passes

Life advanced, and we no longer knew

in which direction the days departed.

We crossed the borders of safety,

no longer dealing with people of little care.

We gathered to ourselves friends few in number,

yet with them we are never wronged.

Sometimes we cling to reasons of the past,

we tire, we part, we suffer, illusions overtake us.

Then we return to the reality of life,

learning our lessons from pain.

Sometimes we rest upon our burdens,

sometimes we rejoice in escaping words.

How strange this world is,

how much it delights in the illusions of life and the sorrows of
days.

What Was, Was

Do not tell me, "We were, we had been."

Do not tell me, "What passed has passed."

No memories are forgotten, no truths denied.

A year returned with no peace, no words.

The heartbeat stopped, taking with it all illusions.

You struck me with arrows of false love.

You left my bed, taking all dreams.

They are not illusions recalled,

but a conscience that died,

and became rubble among rubble.

Nahed Fraitekh

You Are Not Yourself

You are as the moon shining in a cloudy night,

its light hidden behind black mist.

You are as winds tickling a rose on a stormy day,

neither adorning it nor beautifying it.

You are as earth trembling,

not dancing to music's rhythm.

You are not as the soul knew you,

not elegant in speech,

not enchanting indeed.

You are something else,

without taste, without colour.

You are forgetting in all its letters.

You are a grey sky,

a sun distant as November.

Nahed Fraitekh

Accustomed to My Solitude

My solitude possessed me, and I loved it.

I thought I had lost myself in the presence of the one I adored.

Yet her nearness made me feel lonelier still.

I was seized by the sensation of lying upon shifting sands.

And I asked: can I rise again?

Can I escape the pain that has claimed me?

Or will the past devour me, as if I had never been?

I Returned to My Writings

I returned to my writings to pull my soul from your hands.

I returned to my writings to find myself among the folds of
my words.

I returned to my writings to become a butterfly in the sky of
your love.

Words taught me to forget myself in the sanctuary of your
eyes,

and wishes taught me to love you more than myself.

I loved you, my lady, with all my being,

with all my soul, with all my passion for life and more.

Nahed Fraitekh

Nothing Attracts Me

I am astonished; words of love no longer attract me.

Words of love, of memories, of longing—

all are nonsense, lies, hypocrisy.

I am astonished at a heart that no longer beats with joy,

a soul that no longer flies with delight.

Believe me, your memory no longer concerns me.

Nothing Resembles Me

Nahed Fraitekh

Indifference

I claim indifference while drowning in a sea of silence.

The voice of speech is overcome by the silence of thoughts.

No dialogues endure, no reproach avails.

The waves of life cast us adrift,

we wander with the days of age without ecstasy.

We sense joy yet flee toward painful infinities.

It is our life; its terrors entice us.

We run in the circle of time that owns us.

We walk, and the days carry us.

Life passes, and we think we remain,

that we own the universe.

Yet we do not realise the end of life until it comes.

The Other Sky

Sometimes my soul draws me to a sky not my own.

A sky where the spirits of the great and the weak gather.

A sky where the memories of disappointed souls are renewed.

A sky that united me with lovers and beloveds.

And in a corner, I saw those whose hearts were besieged by
hatred,

whose souls were shackled by malice.

All were spirits gathered in one sky.

I felt pity for the faded, wandering souls,

who found no place among lovers nor among haters.

And I asked my soul: where is my place in the second sky?

My soul returned to me, I rose from my dream,

still awaiting the answer.

Nahed Fraitekh

I Asked Myself About Myself

I asked myself about myself,

and wandered through the deep chambers of my being,

searching for my soul —

hoping I might find that little girl again,

the one whose greatest dream was a piece of chocolate

and a song to disappear into.

The child who adored the stars,

who drifted with the hidden planets

as they glimmered behind the clouds,

writing poems she prayed would one day touch the light.

But I could not find her.

I no longer recognise my own reflection,

no longer understand the woman I've become.

I no longer belong to myself,

and I am nothing like who I once was.

Life scattered me across its endless tricks,

so I searched for myself in the ruins of memory —

and there I found her,

hiding in the quiet corners of the past,

clinging, resisting, defying.

Now I dream only of what remains of those memories,

hoping the past will stay,

Nothing Resembles Me

and every burden of this life

will finally fade away.

Nahed Fraitekh

Nothing Resembles Me

I am the forgotten one at the gates of exile.

I am the exiled one at the gates of oblivion.

I am the bitterness of forgotten memories,

the noise of nights without dreams.

Like a stranger I stand waiting beyond the borders of my
homeland,

carrying a broken heart and a foreign soul.

Nothing resembles me, nor my memories.

Even I no longer resemble myself.

Epilogue – The Last Whisper

And now the cantos rest.

The pen has laid down its fire,

the heart has poured its oceans,

the soul has scattered its stars.

What remains is memory,

sweet and bitter,

hope and despair,

truth and illusion.

Love was the path,

freedom the kingdom,

faith the horizon.

O lady of passion,

you were the first and the last,

the impossible and the eternal.

This epic is not an ending,

but a circle returning to its source.

Every word written is a seed,

every tear shed is a river,

every whisper is a prayer.

So let the book close,

not in silence,

but in the echo of eternity:

Love endures, even when all else fades.